The Invisible Her

UNVEILING WOMEN'S INVISIBLE WORK & SPARKING A LEADERSHIP REVOLUTION

Aimee Rickabus

SYNERGY
PUBLISHING GROUP

BELMONT, NORTH CAROLINA

*The Manage Her. Unveiling Women's Invisible Work &
Sparking a Leadership Revolution*
Aimee Rickabus

Published by Synergy Publishing Group, Belmont, NC

Formatting by Melisa Graham

Softcover, May 2025, ISBN 978-1-960892-44-7
E-book, May 2025, ISBN 978-1-960892-45-4

Dedicated to my daughters,
Hannah and Indy Rose

Contents

Introduction..1

Part I: The Wound—Naming Your Gifts

Naming Your Gifts 11

What Do You Want?...15

Why the World Doesn't Need Square Burgers.............19

Child Management..25

Married With Children: A Balancing Act 31

Boundaries and Nice-Girl Syndrome 35

My Journey Into Empowerment 41

Part II: The Shift—Honoring Your Gifts
(and Healing from our Wounds)

Introduction: Shifting the Perspective 49

Creating Your Vision 51

Mother: The Manage Her/The Advantage.................55

Systems Are the Trellis 59

Growing Your Garden: Capital, Systems,
and People 69

Motherhood Teaches Leadership 77

Raised to Fail: The Value of Failing...........................81

Women Solving Problems Is The Way Forward:
The New New 87

Epilogue: Walking with a Ghost—Inspiration
for Your Next Steps...95

Quick Tips & Hacks for Embracing Your
Inner Manage Her...100

Additional Resources...109

Acknowledgments...111

About the Author 113

Introduction

I am the CEO of Tomahawk Information Solutions, which is a value-added reseller of information technology (IT). We sell hardware, software, and services to various companies, from Fortune 500 to Fortune 10. One of our top clients is the second-largest food and beverage company in the world. We're working with several large insurance companies. We work with big oil and gas, as well as many large clients in the automotive industry. We've also grown into the IT space over the last fifteen years. My company did well over eight figures in revenue last year. Not bad for a little mama with six kids and two grandkids.

At the time I am writing this book, I am forty-five years old. I have been a serial entrepreneur since I was twenty-two years old. I started my first company when I bought a piece of real estate and fell in love with flipping 1920s properties. I founded a company that sold the first prenatal protein powder. I started and still have a film and television production company. Actually, I've had two film and television production companies.

I come from a long line of serial entrepreneurs. My father was a professor of business. My mother was the Ernst and Young Entrepreneur of the Year in 1988. She also started the first mail-order pharmaceutical company in the United States. She's a full-blown genius. She was born with spina bifida, so she's a super smart lady who's always used her brain to make money because she knew she couldn't use her body. I learned how to be resilient and think outside of the box at an early age from my parents. (Fun fact: my mom also won an "outside of the box" award at one point in her career!)

I am where I am today because of what I learned from my parents, as well as my own experiences as a serial entrepreneur and CEO. However, a bigger and deeper message has been brewing inside of me. We are in a unique time for women. There are many opportunities that previous generations of women have never had (and worked hard to make possible for current and future generations). As technology is in an exponential growth phase, we are seeing automation, artificial intelligence, and personal devices merge in a way that offers us access to powerful tools. I have realized and want to share in this book that while technology like this can often feel scary, there is a powerful opportunity for women to embrace this technology in a way that only we can. We, as women, relate to the world in very different and unique ways, which I will dive into in the upcoming pages. What if what is happening to us is actually happening for us?

In writing this book, I am honoring my strong woman persona, and I am inviting you along with me! I have realized I need to rise up and be a voice for the voiceless. Part of what has made me strong is, yes, my experience as an entrepreneur and CEO, but it has been my experience as a mother, wife, and Manage Her that has honed my work in the business world. I want every woman to realize that they have a unique set of tools and skills as well. The work we're doing domestically, in our homes, is very much the same work we do when we're leading companies, as far as management organization, inventory management, people management, and capital management go. All of those skills are the same exact thing that we do in a company. People's lives depend on the work we do in our homes, and at home, these skills are never questioned. In the business world, we are often questioned when we implement the same exact skills, often by men.

At home, no one is saying, "Oh wait, I know you just changed that diaper; let me make sure you did it correctly." Yet how many times in a business or leadership setting have we been questioned about how we choose to do something? This is a gender disparity, and I am claiming that we are done with tolerating such nonsense. If you're doing your job well at home, no one even knows you're doing it. It's often only the few moments that you forget something or don't fulfill your usual domestic goddess tasks that people notice, oh, there's no toilet paper. Why is there no toilet paper? How's it possible? What do you mean? There's no milk. So suddenly we have a crisis, right?

I feel like women have been in the position of creating standard operating procedures (SOPs) with homes forever . . . they just don't realize it. We have been operating on budgets, managing capital, managing investments, and managing people: from babysitters to gardeners to the pool guy. We've been doing all of this work, and we do it so well. The concept of this book is to empower more women to join the workforce at the management level, the creator level, and the entrepreneurial level. I want my readers to truly understand how our "invisible work," the household management we all do, has set us up for success in the outer world.

YOU ARE HERE FOR A REASON

Most women and people in general are feeling glum about the prospects of a dystopian future. This book says, "Nope, we (women) are going to rise and assume our rightful seat as not only the CEOs of our household, but also visionary CEOs in the world." I believe the Fourth Industrial Revolution will be the most incredible time for the growth of women the planet has ever seen. The term is attributed to Klaus

Schwab, founder of the World Economic Forum and author of The Fourth Industrial Revolution. He shares that "the Fourth Industrial Revolution has the potential to raise global income levels and improve the quality of life for populations around the world." As our mundane domestic tasks are taken over by digital automation, women will find themselves with more time and mindshare. We will balance the polarities between male and female and restore order to the Earth. I hope this book supports our journey in naming our powerful visionary skills and stepping up to use them in empowering ways.

I have divided this book into two sections. "Part I: The Wound—Naming Your Wound" focuses on helping you see how the patriarchal worldview has systematically oppressed women and made us small . . . up until now, that is! This part of the book aims to make the "invisible labor" that women have been doing for generations not only more visible but also transformative, making the change we want to see in the corporate world. Up until now, the invisible labor has been a wound many women have seen as a detriment to our well-being. Something that has held us back. My goal is to change the invisible work to visible, and part I is going to help us do that. "Part II: The Shift—Honoring Your Gifts (and Healing from our Wounds)" focuses on supporting you in understanding how you can hone and honor the amazing skills you have so you can decide where and how to be a part of the future. This part is intended to inspire a new age of women rising and claiming our seats not only at the current tables but also at the new tables we need to create (that may actually only include women!).

STORIES AND EXERCISES

You will quickly notice that I wrote this book mostly through stories because women are storytellers. I also include writing exercises in the book. Located immediately after the story, they explain the current topic and theme in that part of the book. We have all experienced the exercises in the back of the book, where we have the best of intentions to go back and finish them. Not in this book! I want you to do them as you are reading so you will see the exercises right there, ready to go.

I truly believe that women in leadership change our world. Humans were not built to live in a man's world. And women definitely weren't built to live this way. Now, we have the opportunity to build a world that is for us and by us. I invite you to join me! I'm tired of imitating men. I simply won't do it. So this book is a woman's take on how we can improve the world one woman at a time. My hope is to inspire one woman who can inspire one woman, and so on and so forth. It is my wish that this book can help you get more self-confident, more organized, more self-realized, and more empowered.

Side Note: I am writing this book from my personal perspective, which is as a heterosexual woman who has been married twice. All of my examples and stories are written from these experiences. I acknowledge that there are many other domestic partnerships, perspectives, and circumstances that may differ from mine. However, as I have shared the core messages from this book over the years with many people from a variety of backgrounds, they have found some nuggets of wisdom that they relate to. My hope is that whoever reads this book can see some aspect of themselves and relate to the core messages as well.

Part I: The Wound— Naming Your Gifts

Naming Your Gifts

"You can't really know where you are going until you know where you have been." —Maya Angelou

Women have collective amnesia. You see, we don't remember what life was like for us before the patriarchy. This, of course, was by design, as history is written by the victors, and, well, "he" won. And when he did, he wrote His-Story. Our story (Her-story) was suppressed, hidden away, destroyed.

Our society has been designed by men, for men. And all of the amazing work, accomplishments, and unique history of women often go untold and therefore unnoticed. This is a generational wound many women carry with them, consciously or subconsciously. The wound, as I refer to often in this book, is the psychological wound that women carry due to the long-standing patriarchy. The wound has subjugated women for millennia, in which women were less important than men, had less freedom than men, and historically were even considered as chattel. Until recently, in most Western cultures, women could not vote, could not own property, could not open a bank account, and were not afforded the same equalities and privileges as men. That is a wound we women still carry with us.

We saw that wound in our grandmothers and our mothers, and that wound is carried forward in us. The idea that we are still somewhat subjugated, somewhat still considered less than a man, the idea that we are just pretending to be strong leaders, the idea that we don't really know what we're doing, that's the wound. The wound shows up in our behavior in many ways, like us trying to be nice and make nice instead of taking our lives, and our leadership, and our power back and being full-on equals with men.

The wound is what's left over from systemic subjugation, and the wound still exists today.

The goal of Part I of this book is that we, as women, can name and own this wound by recognizing that it exists. Part of the wound was all of the invisible work that women were given, which had no monetary value and was not considered real "work." I remember hearing a story of my grandfather, talking about my grandmother, saying, "Oh, don't worry, Leeta will do it. She doesn't do anything because she is a stay-at-home housewife." I also remember how much that enraged my grandmother. Stories like these are part of the wound we carry.

The wound is deep, and the wound still exists. Women worked hard with the feminist movements so that they could go out and get jobs, make money, and feel worthy outside of the home. And now, we go out, we do our jobs, and we often come home and get to do our other jobs. The fact that this work is still invisible is a wound. I feel like we're healing. We're getting better with naming it, but it is still a wound.

Until women address these millennia-old wounds, we will never truly heal and find our equal place in an egalitarian society. This part of the book is designed to open our eyes and help us not only notice the amazing work we do every day but also recognize the unnoticed work and help heal the ongoing wounds many of us carry.

Side Note: While I would love to dive into Her-story, for the sake of the book and the overall journey for you as the reader, I simply provide some resources in the "Additional Resources" section at the end of the book, should you want to explore further.

What Do You Want?

Now be honest with me, ladies, when was the last time somebody asked you what you wanted? And meant it?

I actually got to a point in my first marriage where I didn't even know how I liked my eggs cooked. As women, sometimes it's hard not to get lost in pleasing others. We often lose ourselves, our authentic desires, and our authentic gifts.

In this section, we will explore different themes around naming the psychic wounds women have endured during our oppression living in the patriarchy. We will work through exercises that help us name our wounds and rediscover our whole selves. But before we dive in, I want to help you love yourself just as you are. I am giving my permission for you to start liking and loving who you are because that is when we can start living as free people. The patriarchy often uses our self-loathing for so many things, from oppressive mental health to generating sales for large corporations that prey on what you think are your inadequacies. We are done with that, and it starts now.

I give you permission to find your authentic self. To love her and embrace her. To get to know her. To fall in love with her. I want you to write a love letter to yourself. I want you to learn to love yourself more than anyone else. Use the exercise below to help you get started.

EXERCISE: A LOVE LETTER TO YOURSELF

Write yourself a love letter. I really want you to dig deep here. You can start with things you love about your character. Are you tenacious, jolly, smart, funny, lively, resilient, wise, wild, cautious, reserved, outgoing, a good mom, loving, caring, understanding, creative, compassionate, empathic, loyal, honest, optimistic, generous, adventurous, ambitious, patient, curious, analytical, perceptive, open-minded, etc.? List ten qualities you love about your character.

....

....

....

....

....

....

....

....

....

....

....

....

Now, the hard part. We are going to shift to the more surface-level aspects of ourselves, but we are going to find what we love instead of what the world tells us we need to fix or change. What do you love about your body? Imagine that you died. What would you miss most about being in this body? You are just borrowing it. It is temporary. Love it like a bloomed flower, exquisite in its momentary beauty. List five qualities you love about your body. (I am intentionally only asking for five qualities because this is often a more difficult aspect to love, but don't be shy; list more if you can. This is just for you.)

....

....

....

....

....

Why the World Doesn't Need Square Burgers

Women's creativity is so needed in the world. And our invisible labor is a great example of how we regularly exercise our creativity. Up until now, we've been driven by the question "How can I make more money?" versus "How can I improve the world?" Let me share a story that helped me understand this recently. My family was sitting at the kitchen table in our home. It was dinner time, a time when we can all discuss.

My twelve-year-old son looked at me and said, "Mom, I have a great idea."

Me: Tell me, I'm all ears.

Gabe: Ok are you ready? This is big . . . It's a fast food restaurant, but the burgers are square!

Me: Ok, that's very interesting. Let's explore that. But I'm pretty sure Wendy's already has square burgers (patties).

Gabe: Oh . . .

Me: So about forty years ago, that was a great idea! And someone made a lot of money off the Wendy's Burger Franchise. We should see how much they made.

Gabe: Hey, Siri, what's the net worth of Wendy's?

Me: But let me tell you why the world doesn't need square burgers right now . . .

For so long, a common motivation for much of society and business has been, "How can I make more money?" My son illustrated the old, common, patriarchal way of thinking. As he was sharing his "brilliant idea," I thought, "Who is this helping? What societal problem is this solving?" I looked around at the dinner table and thought, "How does this thinking help my other children, their friends, and our neighbors?"

And it hit me: The way I take into consideration my children, our community, and the next generation showed me that my way of thinking is far more expansive and creative than a shiny new product that could make a lot of money. My process shows up in everything I do, from managing my household and making daily decisions to what I put in my kids' lunches and how I wash our clothes. I am guessing, dear reader, that you are nodding along to me right now. Yet, up until now, these daily household decisions and tasks have been viewed as menial and insignificant. I call bullshit! This lack of acknowledging the absolute power of our daily lives—the powerful decision-making, the spending choices, the support we provide—is the wound we carry. Not realizing our collective power as women has held many of us back, but we no longer accept this. By making this small shift and naming the wound, we can start to honor our true gifts.

Here we are on the brink. The world needs our humanity and for us to use our magical superpowers and our creativity. We are going to shift the wound into a gift. Use the exercise below to help you get started.

EXERCISE: NAMING THE WOUND

Name a wound, something you have seen as menial or insignificant up until now:

....

....

....

....

....

....

....

Take a moment and honor that wound. (How did this wound strengthen you?)

....

....

....

....

....

....

Now, acknowledge that this wound can be healed if you are ready for it to be so. And in knowing this, I want you to apply your creativity and write a poem about your wound.

....

....

....

....

....

....

....

....

....

....

....

....

....

....

....

....

....

....

....

....

....

....

....

....

....

....

....

....

....

....

Read it aloud to yourself and understand that wounds plus healing and creativity are transformational! They make us more than what we were before; they deepen and strengthen us.

Child Management

When I decided I wanted to become a mom, it didn't happen right away. But when it finally did, I had a lot of choices to make! The decision-making around pregnancy and birth is much like creating a strategic action plan in business. You have to determine what you want your outcome to be, and you have to figure out how you want to get to that outcome. I'm going to share my journey. Whether you are a mom or not, or hope to be one day or not, the process is similar to other decisions we, as women, make in many other areas of life.

The year was 2008. I had been married for four years and was unable to get pregnant. In August of that year, I had finally done it: I was pregnant, and I was going to be a mom. Yay! Strangely enough, this was the month I began my lifelong practice of yoga.

Now I had someone else to take care of and someone that I wanted more for than even myself. A friend gave me a bundle of books: The Thinking

Woman's Guide to Pregnancy, Water Birth, and The Continuum Concept. I read avidly, like the nerd I am. I ingested data. Based on my research, I made the decision that I wanted to have an at-home birth. You see, it turns out that America is a pretty lousy country to give birth in, so I felt having as much control in my environment would work best for me as my pregnancy was considered low risk. After making my decision, I needed to find a midwife.

In business, we would call this process I went through a "Strategic Action Plan." Put simply, a strategic action plan is where you figure out how you want something to go and then create the strategies to get you there. Here's the thing: You are a visionary. You dare to look into the future and use your instincts, your knowledge, and whatever data you consume along the way to make it a reality. This is planning! You are doing it. You will manage doctor appointments, nutrition, blood tests, and sonograms. You will create a birth plan, choose a place to give birth, and choose your birth class. You, my dear, will be the visionary leader on this journey. Up until now, you just wouldn't get credit for it. Time's up! Women plan, strategize, manage, and lead within their homes, and now it's time to acknowledge and share that visionary work with the world. Let's see that. Let's acknowledge that. You are a born leader. You have been doing it all along.

EXERCISE: STRATEGIC ACTION PLAN

What is one big vision or plan you are working on in your household and life right now? (For example: a big vacation, changing eating habits, pregnancy, prepping for your kid's college journey, buying a house, etc.)

....

....

....

....

....

....

....

What research are you doing (or planning to do) to achieve your vision?

....

....

....

....

....

....

....

What's next? What are the next steps, the steps after that, and then after that?

....

....

....

....

....

....

....

....

....

What do you think or notice now that you have seen how well you created a strategic action plan?

....

....

....

....

....

....

....

....

....

What is the value of this type of planning you are able to do?

....

....

....

....

....

....

....

....

....

Married With Children: A Balancing Act

As you become a mother or caretaker of others, your ability to manage inventory, schedule, plan, and organize in your home will refine itself as your family expands. You also develop your process for maintaining and improving all of the skills you learn. In business, these are called Standard Operating Procedures (SOPs). SOPs are merely the process for when X needs to be done, here's the process for getting X done. For example, I put all the clothes in my deep sink in the laundry room, and when the deep sink is full, I know it's time to do a load of laundry. That's my SOP for laundry. If there isn't enough, the sink is not full (because the sink is about the size of a full drum in the washing machine), and I know I need to wait. If there is too much, the sink is overflowing, and then I know I have waited too long.

There's a reason why women probably know where up to thirty thousand objects are in their home, but your husband or seventeen-year-old driver doesn't know where he left his keys (and you probably do . . . in the pocket of his jeans he left on the bathroom floor last night, right?). I truly believe nature gives women special superpowers around organizing and operating our households that our male counterparts don't often get. I don't want to excuse men from their duties to be equal partners here, but you will find that you (the woman) are simply better suited at doing just about everything when it comes to the management of your home and children. You will generally find that you will be the decision-maker and visionary leader of your family.

I need you to recognize we've been living in a patriarchy that socially conditions women to feel enslaved to our male counterparts. Meaning that they got credit for the work we did, and sometimes we allowed it. This happens all throughout the world, and make no mistake: It is 100 percent based on gender. Our work was their work. However, we can change this by recognizing our past and using it to change our future. The knowledge and skills we as women have used, both historically and currently, have been critical to the survival of our offspring, the next generation. Historically, any knowledge that protected or enhanced the survival of our offspring was typically guarded by the women. Much of our evolutionary survival depended on the woman's ability to manage. We must heal from the historical wound of our superpowers being marginalized and minimized and shed light on and name these as the true gifts they are. We will use our gifts to our advantage and revolutionize and reimagine what we, as women, are capable of. You're welcome, boys!

EXERCISE: IDENTIFY YOUR SOP MAGIC

What is a task you do on a daily or weekly basis in your home? (For example: grocery shopping, laundry, cleaning, etc.)

....

....

....

....

....

How do you know when this task is ready to be executed? (Is there a specific day or some other indicator you use to know when the task needs to be done?)

....

....

....

....

....

....

What is your process for completing this task and
bringing things back to "normal"?

....

....

....

....

....

What do you notice as you answer these questions?
What do you notice about just one of your many
superpowers? How does that make you feel?

....

....

....

....

....

Boundaries and Nice-Girl Syndrome

We have been conditioned to allow people to treat us, as women, in unhealthy ways. We have been conditioned not to name or hold boundaries around things that are important to us. We have been conditioned not to communicate our boundaries and needs.

Ladies, holding boundaries in business management and household management is key to both your personal happiness and your personal success. When we don't honor our hearts, our voices, and our boundaries, we build resentment around the people in our homes and our workplaces.

I'm personally going through this right now. I'm trying to find my voice so that I can hold my boundaries within both my household and my company. This has been a struggle with my business partner, who happens to be my husband. In yoga, we say, "Practice makes practice." In life, this practice is one of my most important and difficult lessons. I have learned I often know what I want, but for some reason, I'm not valuing my own needs at the same level of importance as other people. This is the conditioning that many women have learned: Stay small. Do for others first, at the expense of yourself. Never complain.

Recognizing these behavior patterns within ourselves is key. We must acknowledge when a boundary line has been crossed, even becoming aware when we don't protect our boundaries. This is the process for healing the wound of feeling marginalized and less than. When we don't name, honor, and voice our boundaries, we feel it within our hearts. Then, when we don't say anything with our voices, we reinforce that feeling of inequality, and the cycle continues. What happens if you allow this self-destructive behavior to continue? Your pain turns into resentment on your part. Resentment is an emotion that can then undermine your relationships, both at home and at work. Instead, wouldn't it be better to use your voice to create and reinforce that boundary, to communicate your feelings or needs with the person who has crossed the boundary? Whether it's an employee or your husband or your child, you can make the conscious choice to use your voice (and possibly be a little bit confrontational or a little bit "not nice"). However, the payoff is honoring your worth and equality and avoiding resentment.

The idea that I'm pushing and dealing with right now is nice-girl syndrome. Nice-girl syndrome makes me want to be liked. I don't want to be seen as someone who is confrontational or bitchy or unaccommodating. I fear other people's resentment of me, so I put other people's feelings ahead of my feelings, ahead of my own boundaries. I realize this is probably something that needs to be developed and worked through in order for most women to reach that next level in their careers and in their relationships. It's about finding that next level of communicating your needs without feeling like you are going to hurt someone's feelings.

This practice of honoring and voicing your boundaries can lead to success in areas where you may have missed out on your ability to succeed due to your inability to communicate your personal needs. Failure to communicate effectively leads to resentment on both sides of the fence. When you manage a family or a company, the key to truly succeeding and having happy family members or happy employees is your ability to efficiently communicate what you need from the people around you, setting clear boundaries, clear intentions, and clear SOPs. It is your duty as a Manage Her to make sure there's a very clear line and that you have communicated impeccably what the parameters are for success in each position.

Whether it's your son or the controller of your company, it's the same thing. You want to make sure everybody understands what's expected of them (SOPs) and that when they fall down on those expectations, you are quick to communicate the fact that you see they have fallen down. Then you quickly put them back on track, get them back in line with the SOP, and remind them that mistakes are part of the learning process. The important thing is that they understand the task and can perform it. Honestly, this can be as simple as how to properly import a sales order or how to make your bed. This applies to all the little things.

Communicating calmly and assertively helps you hold your boundaries with the people you interface with in your life. As women and managers, a major part of our people management skills will benefit from reinforcing and communicating these positive and healthy boundaries we have for ourselves.

**EXERCISE: PRACTICING BOUNDARIES
LIKE THE TRUE CEO YOU ARE**

Do a little self-check here. Check in with you. Do you struggle with boundaries?

....

....

....

....

....

....

How does this struggle show up in your daily life?

....

....

....

....

....

How does it make you feel?

....

....

....

....

....

I want you to write the following on sticky notes and put them on your mirror (and I'll do the same).

My feelings and needs are important.

Recognizing my needs and honoring my feelings is good for my relationships.

My Journey Into Empowerment

Sometimes, shifting takes decades. To wrap up part I of this book, naming the wound and recognizing our gifts, I want to acknowledge that you may be feeling a little overwhelmed, a little uncertain, and a little unsure of what's next. I want you to know that is okay! And I'm going to tell you a little story that may seem weird coming from someone like me who seems like a successful and powerful woman now. Here's the thing: It took me eighteen years to transform my life and to transform myself into what I now feel is a fully empowered woman. So don't put me on a pedestal. I'm just a regular girl like everyone else.

I married at the age of twenty-five. I was young. I was cute. I was very successful. I'd been running my real estate business for the last three years and had earned a good fortune. I married a man I thought was the one. He was like Prince Charming. I thought our marriage was going to be roses and dancing in the moonlight. It was not. I don't know exactly what happened. I don't know exactly why it happened. I don't know when it happened. But our relationship devolved into this very, very ugly dance for power. Specifically, his desire for my power. His desire for my light. He thought dimming my light would make his light shine brighter.

I was dealing with existential pain. My pain was a partner that didn't want to see me rise to my potential. Not only did I have a husband who wanted to hold me back, but also I was internalizing the pain so much that I was dimming my own light. I think a lot of women have experienced this. If this is where you are in your life, know that it is okay, and you are still on the journey to making a shift toward your empowerment, even when you can't see the progress.

It was only motherhood that made me eventually leave him. My son was fourteen months old, and the abuse was going from verbal and emotional to physical. I just couldn't do it anymore. So, one day, I was done. I stopped dancing.

That was one of my first experiences with shifting the wound and honoring my power.

FINDING PARTNERSHIP BY LOVING MYSELF

My second marriage started out all right. We'd been friends for years. We knew each other very well, and I thought it would be different this time around. Unfortunately, as our relationship progressed, so too did the power struggle. We basically had a replay of my first marriage, but it played out with way more children and way higher stakes.

Something happened this time that was different for me. I guess I realized that, somehow, I was causing the power struggle. I had the self-realization that somehow I was the problem.

Shit, that self-realization is hard. It's painful. It's jarring. It requires a paradigm shift. I realized I had a lack of boundaries, and I was a high-functioning codependent (thank you, Terri Cole)!

I discovered that the stories I told myself about myself caused me to believe in a version of me that conflicted with my authentic self. I needed to find my power. I needed to find my boundaries. I needed to figure out who I really was. Who am I? What do I deserve? What do I want for myself, not just for my children, but for me? What if I loved myself the way that I loved my children? What if I loved myself like my mother? I was finally exploring and opening up to the idea of serving myself in the highest way. Of loving myself in the most compassionate way possible. In Sanskrit, it's called ahimsa, "non-violence against yourself," or namaha, "honor."

When I found myself, my true self, and truly learned to love her, I came into my full power as a being. And when I brought my fully authentic, unapologetic, fully loved self into my relationship with my husband, something magical happened.

The polarities were balanced. The relationship was balanced. We found mutual respect and love for one another in a way that I've never experienced before. This profound and life-changing experience made my success possible. I began to shift. I realized that I do have something to give to the world that is authentically me. I am a visionary leader in my company and my household. Now, I want to support you in your journey to shift.

Part II: The Shift—Honoring Your Gifts (and Healing from our Wounds)

Introduction: Shifting the Perspective

What if the circumstances throughout your life are not happening to you? What if they are happening for you?

In life, I have found myself in many moments thinking, "Why is this happening to me?" I have absolutely viewed circumstances from a victim mentality. It was only when I shifted my mentality and realized that things were happening for me that I was able to change the trajectory of my life. I began to see actionable changes that I could own, that were my responsibility, and that I didn't need someone else's permission to start changing something that wasn't working. This is the difference between the victim mentality and the winner's mentality. Life is happening for me! This is my personal mantra. I hold it deep in my heart and trust it to be true. It allows me to see the lemons that life hands me as the inventory that fuels my existential lemonade stand.

In part I, we spent time naming the historical wound of the invisible work women have been doing for generations. By naming it, you hopefully have begun to realize this invisible work:

1. Needs to be announced and made visible and
2. Is your superpower.

Now, in part II, we begin the work of shifting perspective to change the trajectory of your life. No more being owned by someone else. We own our lives. If you have been dreaming of stepping into leadership, starting a business, and becoming a true *Manage Her,* this part of the book is going to support you in doing just that.

Remember: "The universe is conspiring in my favor."

Perception is everything. Remember that only in times of pain will you grow. If you are comfortable, you are not growing.

Creating Your Vision

When I was in film school, there were not a lot of women. There were a lot of men. I often found myself struggling to find my way. There was internal and external pressure to "be like the men," and that did not feel good to me. Yet I tried! The first movie I made was called *The Professional*. (I'll pause while you give me side eye here. I know!) Once I embraced the fact that I was one of few, if not sometimes the only, women in film school, I was able to create a film that shed light on a special female filmmaker's plight, wounds, pain, and journey of being in the industry in a time that was dominated by men. Had I not honored my uniqueness as a woman filmmaker, I never could have made that film in the way I did, which happened to win an award.

Recognizing your life circumstances and seeing them as a gift that can solve problems helps you develop a vision for yourself. You have to truly understand a problem to solve it. Part of the shift in honoring our gifts is embracing the awareness of our wounds, trauma, and horrible experiences and understanding how this has given you empathy for people who have similar experiences. Honoring those wounds will help you find your most authentic self and identify your visionary abilities. And when we are operating from the most authentic versions of ourselves, we can recognize the gifts we have for this world. In film school, stepping into my female experiences was my superpower. Now, I invite you to recognize yours.

EXERCISE: CREATING THE VISION

How can we get what we want if we never ask ourselves what we want? This is a creative exercise where we use our imaginations to create new and expanded possibilities for ourselves. Once you have these ideas, meditate on them. Allow yourself to live in that future.

We can use our imaginations in fear mode or love mode. This is your imagination in full love mode as it applies to you. I want you to start visualizing what that looks like for you. I want you to do this exercise as if there were no glass ceiling. Read through the questions to help you name what you want, your vision.

If you could not fail, what would you do?

....

....

....

....

....

If you could do whatever you wanted, what would
you do? Where would you go in the world?
What would you build or create?
Who would you be?
Where would you live?
What would you drive?
What would your relationships look like?
What would that do to the dynamic you have with
your family/children?
How would that change your relationship
with money?
I want you to smell it, feel the air on your skin,
envision your home, and see all the little details. The
more details, the better. Now, write them down.

....

....

....

....

....

....

....

....

....

....

....

....

....

....

....

....

....

....

....

....

....

....

....

....

....

....

....

....

....

....

Mother: The Manage Her/The Advantage

Now it's time to stop seeing yourself as a servant in your house and start seeing yourself as the CEO of your house. The mother of the household typically creates management strategies for everything from how their kids get to school to deciding if, when, and who tutors their children to managing outside employees, like babysitters and house cleaners. When I look around my home, I see a series of decisions that were made by me, from the color on the walls to the type of sofa (and where it is in the room) to the throw pillows . . . everything.

Here's the thing: It's not just the decision-making. It's our thinking and feeling processes as women. We are the true visionaries because we think about how the pillows and the sofa will literally support people when we gather around to watch a movie. We think about how the color on the walls will make us feel when we are at home or when our littlest goes to sleep. Everything we do is so intentional, yet we often don't realize just how intentional we are.

EXERCISE: INTENTIONAL VISION

How do you create your home, family culture, and family traditions?

....

....

....

....

....

Look around your home, pick a spot where you know you have made a lot of decisions, and name every single decision you've made there. More importantly, write about why you made that decision.

....

....

....

....

....

....

....

....

....

....

....

....

....

....

....

....

....

What are you noticing about your intentions for the items in your home? The decisions you make? How do you see that applying to aspects outside of your home?

....

....

....

....

....

....

....

....

Systems Are the Trellis

I also want you to start viewing your home as a business. Let me explain!

In business, systems are used to create processes and procedures that help us operate efficiently and deliver value to both the customer and the organization. Business systems can seem complicated, but women are already well-versed in "business systems"; they just don't call it that. I want to help you make the connection between business processes and terms and the things you do every day in your home.

Let's break this down in terms of the household. You'll see that I share a common business term, and then I'll connect it to examples in the home.

Operational Systems: In my kitchen, I have created a Standard Operating Procedure (SOP) for where my silverware and dishes go. For example, like most people, I put forks in the same place in the same drawer. This creates an operational system so that everyone in my household can return a clean fork to the same spot, and we all know where that is when we need a new, clean fork.

Informational Systems: This is how we use technology. In my home, most of this is done on my phone. I have all my contacts organized so that I can call all the people I manage. I use a calendar on my phone that syncs with my family's devices to manage appointments, tutors, vacation time, school, etc. I use the DoorDash app to order food for my kids when I'm not there. I use the Uber app to move my older kids around.

Communications Systems: Every parent decides when their kids are going to get a phone. What kind of phone? What restrictions are on the device? This goes for tablets and computers as well. But at some point, we need these for internal (within the family) and external (outside the family, like tutors) communications. We use tools like FaceTime with our kids. Our kids use teleconferencing tools like Zoom for educational purposes. We use and implement communication systems within our homes every day!

Financial Systems: I decided on our financial system within the home by choosing a bank based on its app. We all want to be able to do our finances on the go. We pay bills and babysitters with apps like Venmo and Zelle and transfer money to our kids with tools like Greenlight (a game changer for me). Through these systems, we implement systems around our individual financial needs.

Human Resources Systems: This is all about managing the behavioral expectations of the people in our house. Both the "Littles" and the "Bigs" are required to understand rules, boundaries, limitations, and expectations. For example, we all have allowable language. We require "please" and "thank you" to be said when appropriate. We also have repercussions for stepping outside of acceptable standards. In business, this is called an "employee manual." We tell them what is expected of them, such as "make your bed," and they comply or get reprimanded, i.e., "you're grounded."

After reviewing the above business terms, I hope you realize you are the household *Manage Her*. By the way, the average HR manager in the US makes $83,516[1] per year!

I want you to begin shifting. It's fun to realize that the systems within your home save you money and lower your stress. They increase your productivity. They can and should be evaluated at least once per year to take advantage of emerging technologies that can improve your workflow as the *Manage Her* of your home.

---

1. " Human resources manager salary in United States," Indeed, updated April 14, 2025, https://www.indeed.com/career/human-resources-manager/salaries.

EXERCISE IDENTIFYING YOUR MANAGEMENT SYSTEMS

OPERATIONAL SYSTEMS

What operational systems do you use in your home?
What are your SOPs?

....

....

....

....

....

....

....

Could they be clarified or improved? Should you
write them down? Create an employee manual for
your house. Have your family read and sign it.

....

....

....

....

....

....

....

INFORMATIONAL SYSTEMS

These are the apps on your phone. Take a look and write down your most crucial apps for household management.

....

....

....

....

....

....

....

What's new? Let's do a quick search and see if there are new apps that could replace an older app or if there is a new tech gadget (AI tools, like Siri or Alexa) that can help us stay organized or save time. Write them down.

....

....

....

....

....

....

....

COMMUNICATION SYSTEMS

Now, evaluate your current communication systems. How might it be improved? Do you need a family calendar on the wall in the kitchen (old school but effective) or a shared Google Calendar (digital equivalent)?

....
....
....
....
....
....
....

Is it time to put an Alexa or Siri in your kids' room? Would your communication be improved if your kid had a phone? It doesn't have to be a smartphone. Write down your ideas.

....
....
....
....
....
....
....

FINANCIAL SYSTEMS

What are your financial goals? Write them down.

....

....

....

....

....

....

....

....

How could financial systems help you achieve your goals? There are all kinds of apps to help us here, too. Look up a few and write them down here.

....

....

....

....

....

....

....

....

....

....

HR SYSTEMS

Do your people (aka, husband, partner, and/or children) understand how you would like them to participate in household duties? Are they able to understand everything you need from them? If not, you could work with each person to get them to buy in and get excited.

....

....

....

....

....

....

....

....

Name a family member and list the duties and responsibilities that you task this very capable person with. By effectively communicating with each member of your family, you will create a home without resentment (and take the undue burden off yourself). Consider making a Family Handbook for each of your household members (I did this for those over the age of eight). Have them sign it.

....

....

....

....

....

....

....

....

....

....

....

Growing Your Garden: Capital, Systems, and People

Now that we realize how many women manage the systems and SOPs in our homes, I want us to explore how we manage the finances in our homes. This one is huge! Historically, the patriarchal aspects of society made money the "man's" work. Yet, I'm going to guess (just like me) that you've been the "boss" of budgeting, spending decisions, and much more in your household for quite some time. Also like me, I'm guessing you've had to endure financial struggles. Mine happened during my first marriage and first pregnancy . . . extra, right?!

The very same week I discovered I was pregnant with my first child, I started what would become my lifelong yoga practice. Yoga has taught me invaluable lessons about life: how to breathe through discomfort, how to count it out, and to remember that nothing lasts forever. It taught me patience and how to quiet my mind. Over the years, yoga has been a steadfast companion, especially during the toughest times.

In 2008, the world was on the brink of a financial meltdown, and I was feeling the weight of it. Before this moment, I had built a healthy real estate portfolio, and one day, I noticed all my tenants were home in the middle of the day. When I asked them what was going on, I learned their employers had gone out of business as part of the housing fallout. Panic set in immediately. Without jobs, how would they pay rent? And without rent, how would I pay my mortgage? I started to spin, and then I started to get resourceful, something I know you are good at, dear reader!

When the tenants couldn't afford to stay, they moved out, and I pivoted my business model. I started offering short- and long-term furnished rentals, advertising on Craigslist and Vacation Rental By Owner (now VRBO). Times were tight, and people were vacationing closer to home. My hustle paid off, and the new strategy worked.

However, I made a critical mistake. I believed the news when it claimed the government would bail out homeowners and banks would forgive mortgages. I stopped paying mine and saved every dollar, thinking I was making a smart move. Looking back, I realize I'd fallen into a kind of denial. My properties had been sustaining our lifestyle for years, and I had stopped actively focusing on financial reality.

My husband at the time wasn't contributing financially—he'd only worked six months out of our entire marriage. At this point, you may be asking, "How did a girl like me stay in a relationship like this for as long as I did?" Well, the first step was to lose my boundaries completely. Step two was to become highly emotionally codependent. Don't forget to add in denial . . . it's not just a river in Egypt! I didn't want the stigma of divorce, so I just kept on this dark, scary, wrong path. I forgave all transgressions and repressed my true feelings. I didn't want to be judged as a "quitter." If only I had been in touch with the fact that most of my friends and family wanted me to leave him. But I wasn't ready to do that yet. I was still determined to shoulder it all, including the financial burden. I had lost touch with myself, my instincts, and my boundaries.

Then the notice came: My house would be sold at auction the following month unless I paid what I owed. I was eight months pregnant, desperate, and running out of options.

Thankfully, at the time of this financial crisis, I happened to be studying some powerful resources. I was deep into Tim Ferriss's book, *The 4-Hour Workweek*, learning how to work smarter, not harder, and how to maximize my time. As a new yogini, I was also learning how to take my problems to the yoga mat. I had also been exploring the very Zen concept of "beginner's mind" as part of my yoga practice. So in this moment of financial chaos, I quieted my mind and tapped into my "beginner's mind," the part of one's mind that only has curiosity and no preconceived notions; it is brave and full of wonder. I remember the moment the answer came to me so clearly: I needed a partner. I decided to sell 50 percent of the membership in my LLC. How would I find this partner? I posted on Craigslist. (I know, sounds crazy, right? But Craigslist was a powerful technology tool I was using at that time.) And to my surprise, it worked! A lovely couple from Oregon, looking for a second home, stepped in. They had the cash I needed, and we made a deal. While I can now see things I could have done differently, this decision saved my home and got me through a tough time. Looking back, I can see how determined I was not only to get myself out of a tight and stressful financial situation, but also to grow and bloom in new ways. Much like fertilizer helps grow a beautiful garden, stressful moments (okay, really shitty moments!) can help us grow as well.

I also like to think of business principles like a gardener. Capital is the water (fuel), systems are the trellis (structure), and people are the seeds (potential). With the right combination of these three things, you can grow something completely new—something that didn't exist before. This is actually very creative work, very much in tune with our feminine perspective, and very satisfying when it's done properly. Let me break this down using the traditional roles of women in the household.

WE CALL IT CAPITAL, YOU CALL IT CASH

This is the money you have in the bank. This is how we pay rent, buy groceries, and fund our homes. Budgets apply in most households. Do you manage a budget? Do you pay bills? Receive a paycheck? This job duty falls in the accounting department of every company. It's called Accounts Payable and Accounts Receivable, or A/P and A/R for short. In a company, this person's title is "controller." It is a high-level accounting position. The average controller in America nets around $116,831 per year.[2]

Intellectual capital, as it relates to you at home, is your precise knowledge of the systems that get bills paid on time. It takes a ton of creativity to balance cash coming in with borrowed cash, like car payments and credit cards. You are doing amazing financial work, and I want you to see and own these amazing gifts! I also want you to become more financially aware, like the *Manage Her* that you are! Doing so is a very important factor in your overall success and happiness. It is time for us to

---

2. " Controller salary in United States," Indeed, updated April 14, 2025, https://www.indeed.com/career/controller/salaries.

rise. Become more secure in ourselves, become fully aware of our spending, and create opportunities for more financial freedom!

EXERCISE: GROWING YOUR FINANCIAL GARDEN

CAPITAL (AKA: CASH MONEY)
In this exercise, write down how much money you have in the bank.

....

....

....

....

....

After seeing that number, how do you feel about it?

....

....

....

....

....

What technology tools could you implement to manage your money better? Let's do a quick app search and see if there isn't some cool new thing that can help you save money. One of the easiest ways to save is by managing your subscriptions! Write the apps you find here and how you would use them.

....

....

....

....

....

Another very powerful way to manage our money is by getting real about how we spend it. Get your bank and credit card statements, a highlighter, and a ruler. Here we go.

Step 1: Highlight any expense that was unnecessary or frivolous. This is defined differently by each of us. Maybe it's fast food, Starbucks, those shoes we wore one time ever . . . explore any nonessential purchase. You know, the stuff we buy to make ourselves feel better or buy because we are bored.

....

....

....

....

....

....

....

Step 2: Add up the total amount of money you could
have saved or invested differently and write it here.

....

....

....

....

....

....

Step 3: Take some time to reflect on your findings.
Try on a "beginner's mind" and make a note of
anything you want to carry forward as you own your
Manage Her role.

....

....

....

....

....

....

Motherhood Teaches Leadership

Motherhood absolutely develops powerful leadership skills. One example of this is when I started a school. In 2020, during the height of COVID-19, my neighbors became as frustrated as my kids and me with "distance learning," so I hatched a plan. I converted our bonus room into a schoolhouse. I hired a charter school teacher whose school just got defunded. I found a curriculum suitable for first through sixth graders and formed a pod. In the fall, we started the school and named it Travelers Academy. It became such a fun school year!

All of this strategic thinking around problem-solving and deciding to create something different are all examples of what a leader does. I just saw an article that said a top manager's best quality is attentiveness. Women are super attentive and in tune with the needs of those around them, especially their children. This is called emotional intelligence in the business world. Women have it in spades!

Once we got organized and fully implemented the plan I designed for Travelers Academy, we wound up with ten kids learning and growing in ways that worked for them. Motherhood hones our *Manage Her* skills by forcing us to be leaders to our children. It reinforces our ability to plan, strategize, adapt, use our emotional intelligence, and garner the fullest sense of attentiveness. I am not alone in this thinking! Jaclyn Margolis, PhD, and faculty member at Pepperdine Graziadio Business School, shares the following insight in a *Psychology Today* article: "Once I started looking for signs of work-family enrichment in my own life, I realized that becoming a mother gave me a crash course in several things that made me better at my job, ranging from a new perspective on life to acquiring unique skills." In her article, "Lessons in Leadership From Motherhood," she explains how more research has surfaced exploring the correlation between motherhood and personal and professional growth.[3]

_____

3. Jaclyn Margolis, PhD, "Lessons in Leadership From Motherhood," *Psychology Today*, posted November 3, 2023, https://www. psychologytoday.com/us/blog/shifting-workplace-dynamics/202311/ lessons-in-leadership-from-motherhood.

You may not have had to start a school out of your home, but I am guessing your journey as a mother or caregiver has taught you many valuable lessons. It's powerful to think of how those valuable lessons can uniquely transfer into leadership roles outside of the home. Women are uniquely qualified to lead, so let's start doing just that!

EXERCISE: MAKING THE MOTHERHOOD AND LEADERSHIP CONNECTION

As a mother and/or caregiver, list any and all things you do to take care of your loved ones.

....

....

....

....

....

....

....

....

....

....

....

....

Now, take that list and identify the leadership skills used in each of the above items.

....

....

....

....

....

....

....

....

....

....

Finally, reflect on how you might apply these skills in your current and/or future leadership roles.

....

....

....

....

....

....

....

....

Raised to Fail: The Value of Failing

It's 1988 in sunny Southern California. My mother was a powerhouse, often up before the sun. If I wanted to spend time with her, I would get up early and sit in her bathroom while she got ready for work. Her walk-in closet was full of power suits and expensive-looking high heels. Her nails were always done. She would apply false eyelashes methodically every morning. She always said eyelashes gave her "her mojo." Her curly blonde hair was set with hot curlers and then brushed out, a coif of blond hair. She always wore a full face of makeup, eyeshadow, blush, and red lips. She would wear a signature scent, which changed a few times over the years. I think it was Ralph Lauren at the time. She always looked fit, though she never worked out. Instead, she had these machines in her bathroom. I think they were from the '60s. One was some sort of exer-cycle with rollers that you would lean against as it spun around your body. Her favorite place to hang out was in the jacuzzi. We would often sit there at night and do a recap of the day. You see, my mother was a visionary. The way she presented herself and her daily routines was a part of what supported her in that vision.

She envisioned a future where everything you needed could be delivered directly to your home. She was a pharmacist and often wondered why people had to waste their time standing in line at the pharmacy to get prescriptions refilled every month. As my mother would say, "A colossal waste of time!" Honestly, she was just about thirty years ahead of her time. I mean, think about it: Amazon delivers everything now. She could have been Jeff Bezos.

During American Prescription, the name of her pharmaceutical company, we had two BMWs in our driveway. My mother had a beautiful office building that contained a forklift and a huge warehouse. My mother used barcodes to keep track of all the different prescription bottles in her pharmacy. This was before the widespread use of barcodes we know today. Her pharmacy was the first one to implement barcodes. She was innovative that way. I remember she had one room that was just a massive computer. In another room, she had these amazing little machines that would count pills and automatically put them into bottles. It was all very futuristic. Her company filled all the prescriptions for a large health insurance company. She had figured out all of the logistics and created something entirely new.

In 1989, my mother was awarded the Ernst and Young Entrepreneur of the Year Award. I was nine years old, and I was so proud to be at that event watching my mom receive her award. It was a very inspirational moment for me. Yet, by 1990, my mother would be bankrupt. In some ways, it felt like Icarus flying too close to the sun. My mother never talked about exactly what happened—I think it was just too painful for her. Perhaps the world wasn't quite ready. You see, in our house, it was okay to fail, but dwelling on failure wasn't allowed. If you failed, it was your job to get back up and try something else.

My mom was a living masterclass in perseverance. She demonstrated, time and again, how to never give up. Whenever she failed, she got back up and kept going. Through her, I learned a valuable lesson: Failure is an option, but it's not the end of the road. As my husband often says, "Flush it and move on."

Later in 1989, she was offered four million dollars in an 80/20 split by a Wall Street firm. My mother's tragic mistake was that she did not take the deal. She was confused, not a lawyer, and not savvy on Wall Street. At that moment, she was a deer in headlights and did not honor her boundaries.

She wasn't efficiently communicating what she wanted and looked to others instead of owning her preferences. All it took was a series of bad decisions, and by 1990, her company was gone.

Ladies, we can all learn from this. We must stand strong as leaders and make wise decisions based on the facts we have at hand and what we truly want. Resilience is one of life's greatest allies. I've relied on it countless times to overcome challenges. In my experience, this single quality is foundational to any person's success.

I visited the park a few months ago with my friend Blair and our kids. As we chatted, she pointed out a key difference in our upbringings. Her parents focused on avoiding failure, while my mom taught me how to fail—and, more importantly, how to bounce back. That conversation stuck with me because it highlighted a truth we often overlook: Rarely do we do things perfectly, especially when we're learning something new. Failure is part of the process.

We must learn to accept starting as beginners, embrace what we don't yet know, and adopt a mindset of openness, curiosity, and freedom from preconceived notions. I love this concept because it frames life as an ongoing adventure.

Challenges are inevitable, and women know this better than anyone. As a *Manage Her,* we have special abilities and opportunities (if we choose to see them as opportunities) to explore, learn, and grow. Each day is its own little adventure, and embracing that perspective can make all the difference.

EXERCISE: OWNING AND GROWING FROM FAILURE

Write about a time when you felt like you failed at something (maybe as a parent, a spouse/partner, at work, etc.).

....

....

....

....

....

....

How might you view this "failure" differently? What did you learn from it? How did you grow from it?

....

....

....

....

....

....

Where are you not owning your power and *Manage Her* skills? How is fear of failure holding you back?

....

....

....

....

....

....

....

Women Solving Problems Is The Way Forward: The New New

Women have a unique perspective. We account for up to 80 percent of consumer spending.[4] If women tap into the market by addressing business issues in the powerful ways they solve problems in their everyday lives, then we have a revolution in the making.

As I write this part of the book, I'm driving in my car and talking into the notes app on my phone. I just had the most fantastic meeting of the minds with a group of twenty- and thirty-year-old

---

4. Kate Daugherty and Melinda Sineriz, "Male vs. Female Spending Statistics [2025]: Who Spends More?" FinanceBuzz, updated August 7, 2024, https://financebuzz.com/male-vs-female-spending-statistics.

entrepreneurial philanthropists. I am struck by a feeling of ecstasy. A feeling of love for the people on this planet, this beautiful flying zoo that's hurling through outer space at twenty thousand miles per hour. I'm struck by the fact that I'm here right now at a very pivotal time in human history, where we stand on the brink of extinction in many ways. Yet I am filled with hope. We are already living in a pretty phenomenal age, but I can only imagine what technology is going to do for us in the next six years.

I believe that, in the right hands, technology can save humanity and this planet. That empowerment of men and women by the Fourth Industrial Revolution brings balance back to humanity, and therefore, to the Earth itself. I want to reiterate that this book is not about being better than men. This movement is about gender parity. This book is about finding your power to contribute to this effort. I believe women's empowerment will help men find their balanced masculine energy and that the relationship between men and women is reciprocal. Women must name the wound and heal quickly, as there is no time for anger. We need to make the future right now with love in our hearts towards all beings.

We have unpacked all the amazing ways women nurture and maintain their homes, families, and lives. We began connecting the dots between those amazing skills and how they can be implemented as *Manage Hers* in the entrepreneurial, creative, and corporate world. Now, consider how the growth of technology can support our endeavors as well. It can simplify our lives and give us even more space and time to make the impact we want in the world. How can you implement new technology to benefit your life right now?

Let's face it: I work. I know you work too! I fought against implementing AI and other technology into my home until my amazing success coach, Malika, turned me around and had me get Alexa for every room in my house. Now I can wake up my kids from anywhere, drop in on them if they aren't answering their phones, and buy what I need while cooking dinner with only my voice. Alexa even reminds me when I'm getting low on laundry soap!

What if you could do good while embracing technology and your amazing *Manage Her* skills . . . and make a living doing it? I've been part of conversations with some of the most visionary entrepreneurs of this age, where they share beautiful visions of the future. Their ideas are transformative and powerful, where the desire to help humanity is held at a higher principle than personal gain. The innovative technology this group of visionaries is producing will change the world for the better, and I'm talking about revolutionary change that will happen within this decade. No matter who you are, I want you to be empowered to find your voice. The world needs thoughtful women like you, so decide how you want to be a part of the future.

Women are natural problem solvers. As I've shared in this book, we see inefficiencies, gaps, and things that must be fixed. Women easily identify issues and are solution-oriented. Some of the biggest companies today were built by women solving everyday problems.

Look at Skims. Kim Kardashian is a curvy girl who understood the limitations of shapewear. It's a billion-dollar company!

Bumble, created by Whitney Wolfe Herd, allows women to message first and choose the men they engage with on the app, giving women more control over dating.

My friend, Ioanna Mantzouridou Onasi, is a young CEO who uses AI for microlearning. Her company, Dextego, is a cloud-based software platform that uses microlearning to teach sales teams better soft-sell techniques. Microlearning creates educational prompts that are specific to the individual.

Unicorn is just getting started, but I think it's a fantastic idea by a woman named Denielle Finkelstein. She's putting tampon dispensers in bathroom stalls. (Why wasn't that already a thing?)

Despite these examples of women solving important problems, "Only 1.9 percent of venture capital funding goes to women-founded startups."[5]

---

5. Lindsey Allard, "Women's Access To Capital: Overcoming Challenges And Finding Opportunity," Forbes Finance Council, *Forbes*, posted March 7, 2024, https://www.forbes.com/councils/forbesfinancecouncil/2024/03/07/womens-access-to-capital-overcoming-challenges-and-finding-opportunity.

But it's not because we're not good at business. It's because, unfortunately, the banking system wasn't built to fund us, and that's why we need to be bold. We must demand funding, invest in each other's ideas, and build businesses that shift the old model.

**EXERCISE: SOLVING THE PROBLEMS
BY CREATING THE ANSWERS**

Take a couple of deep breaths and allow your mind to be wide open to possibilities. Take inspiration from this chapter. What does the world need? What do you know that other people don't? What's your New New? We must create our way out of destruction. The answers lie within us all.

What do you think are the most pressing issues for humanity right now?

....

....

....

....

....

....

....

....

What are your most pressing issues right now?
What's hard? What's not working?

....
....
....
....
....
....
....
....
....

If you knew you couldn't fail, could you come up with
a creative answer to this problem in the world?

....
....
....
....
....
....
....
....
....
....

If you knew you couldn't fail, could you come up with a creative answer to this problem in your own life?

....

....

....

....

....

....

....

....

....

How can you explore implementing these ideas as a real possibility? Who do you need to talk to? What do you need to do next?

....

....

....

....

....

....

....

....

....

Epilogue: Walking with a Ghost—Inspiration for Your Next Steps

My family visits Kauai all the time, specifically the North Shore. There's something about that place that draws us back again and again, like a gravitational pull. We've built friendships there, and in 2024, one of our friends arranged for us to stay at a stunning house overlooking Hanalei Bay.

We travel with our five younger children and a nanny, so we need a big house. The owner, who recently lost her husband, hadn't visited the house much since his passing. Knowing the circumstances, I went in expecting there might be an energy in the house—some sadness lingering in the air, something that needed clearing. I didn't think much of it, as I've experienced and even navigated feeling this kind of energy before, so I just planned to enjoy our time in the gorgeous home.

The house was breathtaking, with jaw-dropping views of the bay, lush waterfalls, and towering mountain ranges. The lawn was enormous, the pool gorgeous, and everything about it radiated elegance. But as beautiful as it was, we all felt the sadness hanging in the air. It wasn't heavy, just a quiet echo of a presence that hadn't fully moved on. I sensed the energy was that of the late husband.

The first day, I felt his presence faintly. It was as though this place had been his sanctuary, his special corner of the world. I understood why his wife hadn't been back much—it was probably still too raw for her. The next day, my husband and son flew to Oahu with our friend for a jiu-jitsu competition, leaving me with the other kids at the house. I took some time for myself and went to a yoga class nearby while the kids played at the house with our nanny. At the end of class, while lying in Savasana, I suddenly felt a wave of emotion wash over me. Tears streamed down my face as I sensed him, the late husband, again. I felt a strong pull from him, almost begging me to deliver a message to his wife: He wanted her to know that he loved her so very much. He loved their kids so much. And he was still here, still watching over them.

When I got in the car, inspiration struck like lightning. For the first time in months, I started writing again. It was as if this energy had cleared my writer's block, urging me to finish a book I had been drafting on and off for a few years. It was a book about the power of women and the unpaid labor we do, but I didn't really understand what I was trying to write yet. The fact that I was suddenly thinking about this vague book again created a powerful moment, and it made me very curious: Who were this guy and his wife? What was I supposed to learn from them?

Later that night, after putting the kids to bed, I had some quiet time. Earlier, I'd discovered the Sonos system in the house and tried to connect my Pandora account, but the only music available was his playlists. So I decided to play them, tuning into his energy, his vibration, and his essence. I began writing more as I listened, feeling inspired but not understanding why. Finally, I did some digging and was able to find his name. After a little research, I discovered this man, the late husband, had been an incredible entrepreneur, a "Top 40 Under 40" kind of guy who built a fortune with a brilliant idea. He met his wife in college, and together, they had three beautiful sons. Tragically, in 2015, he was diagnosed with cancer. He battled bravely for eight long years before passing on December 3, 2023—coincidentally, my forty-fifth birthday. He was also forty-five when he passed. Then it all started to click.

As I learned more about him, I could tell that in his lifetime, he subscribed to the typical patriarchal male ideology. He took a lot of credit for the work his wife did during his lifetime, and she allowed that to happen. It seemed like he minimized his wife's contributions to the company, which I discovered they had built together. He was allowing his ego to make her feel small and unimportant when, in fact, she was the marketing mind behind his very successful company.

The energy I sensed from him was quite different from what I had learned about his past. It was as though he was very much able to see what he had done to her. I kept feeling like he wanted to tell her how powerful she really was (and still is!) and how important her work was, both inside and outside the home, to the success of their company. Not just his company, but their company. Maybe in his limited experience, he could not fully embrace the idea of egalitarianism, or equality in their marriage. I quickly realized why we had been divinely guided to stay in this house and why I was sensing his perspective, his clarity, and his urgency: It was actually for her, his wife, and I believe, for all women.

This experience reminded me of my legacy and the shortness of life. This is how *Manager Her* came about, not because of him, but because I knew he finally recognized all the invisible work his wife did. As I wrote, I felt that guiding presence. I crafted a chapter about motherhood and the powerful managerial skills it instills. I started seeing life and the work women do not as a series of obligations or stresses but as a gift, an opportunity to make a difference.

Walking with his presence (and thus, indirectly, his wife's presence) during those days reminded me to live courageously. To take risks. To show my loved ones how much they mean to me. And to leave a mark—not for fame or glory, but for the sake of posterity, the people I love, and those who may draw inspiration from my story.

We don't have all the time in the world. As Jim Morrison said, "Nobody here gets out alive." But if we embrace life with the clarity of someone who knows how short it really is, we can make it extraordinary. This experience broke my writer's block and reignited my passion. It reminded me that our time here is brief but powerful and that it's up to us to make it count. I hope this book leaves an imprint of myself, all the women who have come before me, and all those who will come after me. Most importantly, I hope the book makes a dent in crafting a world where all of the *Manager Hers* use their powerful gifts in the ways only women can!

Quick Tips & Hacks for Embracing Your Inner Manage Her

There are so many ideas I have learned for myself and observed in others over the years that can help women own their inner *Manager Her*. But if I included them all in this book, it would be hundreds of pages too long! When I'm hired as a speaker, the audience loves these simple, effective ideas they can implement immediately. So I created a section of quick tips and hacks for shifting your mindset and honing your *Manager Her* skills! Feel free to come back, reference, and use them over and over.

ADJUST AND CONQUER

I'm constantly bobbing and weaving. I have learned to use my intuition to know when something is wrong and, more importantly, do something about it. To make something better, first you must realize you have a problem. Women often sense when something is off but don't honor that nudge. One example of adjust and conquer in our home is when activities overlap for each child. We often break the schedule down and figure out who will take responsibility for each activity. This includes driving the kids, making sure they have their equipment, their snacks, their water, etc. At work, the biggest use of adjust and conquer happened during COVID. Mohawk, our other IT company, made a big shift in directly supplying mission-critical data center infrastructure to Fortune 500 companies since the supply chain was completely shut down. We had to get permission directly from a large manufacturer to do this, but we did it the right way, and they appreciated us stepping in to help when there was nothing they could do for their customers. And with Tomahawk, we did a big pivot during COVID, and instead of selling IT, we supplied a large railroad company with a railcar full of hand sanitizer that we sourced from a spice manufacturer in Southern California. Adjust and conquer is about getting done what you need to get done, figuring out how to do it efficiently by shifting your mindset, and understanding that there's always a way. And, if the way isn't working, then you must identify it and change it. Here is a quick process for shifting this and making "adjust and conquer" your new MO (modus operandi).

- Step 1: What's wrong? Identify the issue, problem, inefficiency, etc.
- Step 2: How can we adjust and make changes? Explore all the options you can think of.
- Step 3: How does this change "conquer" that problem? What does it look like when that problem is resolved?
- Step 4: Now that you've implemented the change, how is it working? Repeat the above steps if needed.

I use this exercise inside and outside my home. It works equally well for both.

PRETTY LITTLE IDEAS BOOK

The "Pretty Little Ideas" book is a habit I started doing for myself in 2003. I have a pretty journal I use for my business ideas. I use it to capture any ideas that show up for me, and here are just a few I captured:

- New product
- Book idea
- Piece of art I'd like to create
- Business strategy for my company
- Real estate deal I'd like to do
- Idea for a new company

- Logo design or a marketing strategy

I don't censor myself, and this book is where I can put all those ideas without any judgment. This is where you, too, can brainstorm free from outside critique. Just allow yourself to flow freely in this journal. Even when I have no ideas showing up, sometimes I just doodle in it, and that's great too.

I was going through my "Pretty Little Ideas" book the other day, and I noticed so many diverse ideas! It is very fun to have an archive of your creativity, and it's always neat to look back and see where an idea started when it grows into something big. Of course, not every idea you write down in this book will come to fruition, and that's okay. So get yourself a cute little notebook or keep it in your Notes app on your phone. Write down any little business or creative ideas you might have. Let your creativity and imagination run wild!

CAIN'T NEVER COULD

My grandmother, Leeta, used to say, "Can't never could," except in her thick Oklahoma accent, it sounded more like, "Cain't never could!" This phrase has stuck with me and has been a powerful mindset tool because those little voices inside your head are powerful! They will try to stop you, even when you want to do amazing things. You need to have a stronger will, know you are on a mission to fulfill your destiny, and know that when you accomplish your goals, you move the entire glass ceiling for those near and dear to you. Recently, I was lying in bed, trying to convince myself that I simply could not make it to my writing call at 7:30 a.m. to work on this book. Honestly, this annoying little voice was trying to convince me that it was, in fact, impossible for me to be on that call. While in my mental battle, I listened to a special recording from my amazing success coach, Malika, focused on "finding your voice." Her wise words gave me the motivation to at least get up and make my usual latte in the kitchen. While standing in the kitchen, I heard my Gram's words, "Cain't never could," and I made it to the call. If I had not leaned on these wise women and my willpower, I don't think I would've come to the call at all. If you've already convinced yourself that you cannot do something, then, my dear, you never will. You are the decider. If you want to be able to do something, you also have to be willing to shift your mindset into a place of believing that you can do it. Using our imagination to believe in our ability to do something is a powerful tool. A lot of people call this manifesting. The simple shift in your mindset from can't to can is essential. In our culture, we often look for the most complicated answer. When in fact, it is the most simple. Yes, you can. Often, the only person who will ever hold you back is you.

MAKING MOLEHILLS OUT OF MOUNTAINS

Turning big things into little things is a mindset shift that can level you up. The idea is to trick your mind into making any task seem as easy as buying milk at the grocery store so that no matter what needs to be done, you can and will do that task with as much ease as possible. This strategy is also about creating a healthy habit of not turning molehills into mountains. You see, our minds love to overcomplicate things and make excuses for why we can't do something (see "Cain't Never Could" as a reminder!). For example, I have just been tasked with helping a friend get her software company implemented at a large food and beverage company. It's a big project, and I already have a lot on my plate as a *Manage Her.* I could freak out, turn it into a mountain, decide there's no way it can be done, and make reasons why it won't work before I even try. Or I can look at it step-by-step, use some of the tips and hacks I've shared in this book, and see what is within my control and ability to do. I can set a meeting with my VP of global sales, so he can learn about her software product. Then I can see how viable he finds her product for this company. Making mountains into molehills is all about starting with small steps, which progress into other small steps. I love my mother's saying, "There is nothing to it but to do it." The habit to create here is to see all things as a series of small steps.

DO WHAT YOU LOVE

My dad always said, "Do what you love, and you will never work a day in your life." This phrase was originally coined by Mark Twain, and I know it sounds cliche, but when you follow your passion rather than money or fame, you will find you are always the right person for the job.

When you do what you love, it is easy to stay focused and engaged. You wake up excited to participate in your life. So when you are being creative in your "Pretty Little Ideas" book or out pitching an idea, be sure it resonates with you deeply. Check with your heart. Make sure that this thing absolutely must be done, that there is no other way, and that you feel mission-driven. Having that sense of urgency and intensity about a project helps it get off the ground. It gets other people excited about what you are doing. And when other people like what you are doing, they want to be a part of your mission. They will want to follow your clear and beautiful vision. For me, this has worked time after time, whether it's flipping a 1920s house, making a movie, launching Mamalicious (the world's first prenatal protein), launching a podcast, or writing this book! Your enthusiasm and love for what you do and put out in the world are the greatest tools in your success quiver.

THE POWERFUL TO-DO LIST

Most of us know and use a to-do list as a tool to help us complete our tasks and goals. This is a very efficient way to hold yourself accountable for what you accomplish each day. It is also a good way to avoid procrastination. I learned about making powerful to-do lists from my mother in my early twenties, and I learned a very interesting trick to make the list work even better for me. Any task for my to-do list I really, really didn't want to do would go in the number one position on my list. If you do the hardest thing first, everything else is easy. I'm a fan of a physical notebook for to-do lists . I know it's super old-school, but the most successful times in my life have been when I've used a spiral-bound notebook for my powerful to-do list. In fact, I was just going through my filing cabinet, and I have spiral-bound notebooks going back more than twenty years!

Whether you have a paper notebook that you run chronologically for dates with all your tasks and daily notes (like my mother taught me) or use the Notes app on your phone to make and prioritize your to-do list, it is an important tool for success. Lists are essentially time and task management, so find the process that works best for you and stick to it!

BOX BREATHING

Learning how to really breathe and feel your breath is a wonderful way to shift from a state of frenzy and worry to a state of present and calm. Box breathing is simply a way to count out equally for an inhale, a pause, an exhale, and a final pause. Here's how I do it (and you can do this with me):

- Take a moment and sit comfortably. Relax your mind.
- Breathe deeply through your nose for a count of five and hold your breath for five.
- Now, breathe out for a count of five and hold at the end of the exhale for another count of five.

This "box breathing" calms the nervous system. You can use this technique anytime you need to calm or steady yourself. This technique helps shift your mind and body in powerful ways.

Additional Resources

Below are some of my favorite books and resources that have taught me many lessons along the way:

- *Women's Bodies Women's Wisdom* by Dr. Christiane Northrup
- *The War of Art* by Steven Pressfie
- *Rich Dad Poor Dad* by Robert Kiyosaki
- *Seven Spiritual Laws of Success* by Deepak Chopra
- *4-Hour Workweek* by Timothy Ferriss
- *The Female Brain* by Louann Brizendine
- *The Thinking Woman's Guide to A Better Birth* by Henci goer
- *Dancing Naked in the Mind Field* by Kary Mullis
- *The Big Leap* by Gay Hendricks
- *Boundary Boss* by Terri Cole

HERSTORY REFERENCES:

- "Lessons in Leadership From Motherhood" by Jaclyn Margolis, Ph.D. (Psychology Today,

November 3, 2023): This article discusses how motherhood can be a source of personal growth, both in personal and professional lives, highlighting leadership lessons from parenting such as generous interpretation, why-asking, and transition management.

- "Phyllis Schlaly" by Arbora Johnson (National Women's History Museum, 2022), www.womenshistory.org/education-resources/biographies/phyllis-schlafly

Acknowledgments

I want to thank my family for being the mirror that reflects me back to me. I love you all too much. My husband, Brenden. My sons Julian, Gabriel, Daniel, and Paul. My daughters, Hannah and Indy Rose. You all inspire me to be a better human everyday.

My therapist, Dr. Piper Walsh, a visionary feminist, who asked me to write down everything I do for my household and then compare that list with my husband, thus unveiling my invisible labor.

To SCMSDC who chose me to do the RISE Program sponsored by SoCal Edison, it was that curriculum that got me thinking about how strategic action plans, capital, people, and systems management all applied to our households.

To WBENC for fighting for gender parity for the last twenty years and to all my WBE sisters, I see you.

Also to Kym Sawtelle, my writing partner of eight years, you have taught me the secret history of women. Knowing the truth about the history of women has been monumental in understanding where we have been and where we are going. I appreciate your wisdom.

To my friend, Quentin Thomas, who just last week spoke words that brought me this epiphany.

To Ioanna Mantzouridou Onasi, who as a futurist saw how automation was going to also apply to the mundane tasks of the household.

To my entrepreneur friends—L.R. Fox, founder of The Oasis, Will Mamer from Save the Bees, Ioanna Mantzouridou Onasi of Dextego, Wendee Close of Goals 2 Life, Nikki Bostwick of The Fullest—I just want to say thank you for sharing your vision of the future with me. Thank you for giving me hope for humanity. Thank you for showing me that the balanced masculine and balanced feminine energy is already aligning, and that the change is already happening. Your beautiful visions of the world represent both the best aspects of the collective.

About the Author

Aimee Rickabus is a mother of six, a business owner, and the voice behind *The Manage Her* podcast. As her family grew, so did her responsibilities—and with them, her capacity to manage more. She found herself leading everywhere: from business meetings to homeschooling lessons, managing teams and timelines, emotions and energy. The more she carried, the more she realized that what she was doing wasn't just multitasking—it was leadership.

But no one was calling it that.

The Manage Her was created to change that. It's a movement to turn the invisible labor women do every day into something visible, valuable, and shared. Through her book, podcast, and platform, she's helping women recognize that the way they manage their homes, their teams, and their lives is leadership—and it's time we started treating it that way.

Connect with her at TheManageHer.com or on Instagram @aimeerickabus and @themanageher.